Rock] to spot

Illustrated by Stephanie Fizer Coleman
and Dave Kurtz Williams

Designed by Jenny Addison and Ruth Russell
Words by Simon Tudhope

You can use the stickers to fill in the chart
at the back of the book and keep track
of the wildlife you've seen.

Fish

Rock goby

This little fish clings to rocks using suckers on its lower fins so it doesn't get swept away by the tide.

Shanny

A shy fish that hides under rocks and seaweed. It can survive out of water at low tide, but will leap straight back in if disturbed – which is why it's nicknamed the 'sea frog'.

Rock gunnel

Look carefully and you might spot this fish weaving through the stones and seaweed, its flat body rippling like a ribbon.

Long-spined sea scorpion

An aggressive rock pool predator with a large, toad-like head and golden 'bug' eyes. It can swallow prey as big as itself.

Shore rockling

Try gently lifting stones or parting seaweed to find this long, brown fish. It uses its three whisker-like barbels to find food.

Fins move in a continuous wave motion

Shore clingfish

A glistening, leech-like fish that clings to rocks to avoid predators. It has a flat body and a streamlined head, so the tide just washes over it.

Fish

Feeds on rock barnacles

Montagu's blenny

Look for a slender fish with pale blue spots all over its body. It can survive out of water at low tide, and avoids scavenging gulls by hiding under rocks or seaweed.

Sea stickleback

In early summer, watch for this fish darting in and out of bladder wrack seaweed, where the male builds a nest and guards the eggs.

Male fans his eggs to keep them clean

Corkwing wrasse

One of the jewels of the rock pool, this colourful fish isn't hard to spot. It's used in fish farms to clean salmon, because it eats the lice that live on their skin.

Lumpfish

This soft, pudgy fish lives out at sea, but returns to coastal areas to breed. Its eggs are used as a cheaper version of caviar.

Mermaid's purse

These are the empty egg cases of sharks, skates or rays. They can be carried into rock pools by the tide. If you find one with curly tendrils at the top it will be a shark's.

Worm pipefish

A long fish with a little snout like a sea horse. It's easily mistaken for a strand of seaweed, so remember it's always worth getting down for a closer look!

Jellyfish and starfish

Common starfish

A familiar sight on the seashore, this starfish has pale spines along its arms. It's often found near mussels, which it prises open to eat.

Colour varies from orange to green or grey

Cushion star

Keep your eyes peeled for this small, plump starfish tucked under rocks. It has short arms and feeds at night.

Spiny starfish

A big starfish that can grow to the size of a dustbin lid. You might see it with one arm shorter than the others, because (like all starfish) it can lose and regrow limbs.

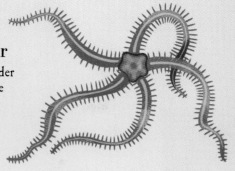

Common brittlestar

Most likely to be found under the stones in rock pools. Be careful not to touch its long arms, because they're very fragile.

Compass jellyfish

Can be left stranded in rock pools in the summer months. Watch out for its tentacles – they give a nasty sting.

Moon jellyfish

A common jellyfish seen all year round. It has four pale circles inside its bell, and doesn't sting humans.

Seaweeds

Bladder wrack

One of the most common sights on the seashore. It has pairs of air 'bladders' to keep it upright in the water, and is fixed to rocks by a large root-like stem.

Rainbow wrack

This is also called 'magic seaweed' because it looks brown when out of the water at low tide, but when the sea returns it shimmers with turquoise, indigo and violet.

Sea oak

This seaweed has fronds like red oak leaves. You can find it growing on rocks or the stalks of larger seaweeds.

Coral weed

You can spot this around the edges of rock pools. Its fronds are stiff and rough, because they contain the same substance that makes shells (calcium carbonate).

Fronds have white tips

Sea lettuce

A bright green seaweed that you'll often see floating on the water. Its fronds are so thin you can see through them.

Gutweed

A very common seaweed with thin, air-filled fronds that sway in the water like long grass.

9

Molluscs

Edible periwinkle

This sea snail grazes on algae-covered rocks. It can be found in large numbers, and is cooked and sold as a seaside snack.

Shell colour varies depending on the food it eats

Dog whelk

You're most likely to spot this sea snail near its favourite food – barnacles and mussels. It bores through their shells and sucks them out through the hole.

Cockle

Look for cockles in rock pools with sandy bottoms. They're a popular snack for birds and crabs, and also humans.

Mussel

Mussels live in large groups attached to rocks. They're often exposed when the tide goes out, and attract many predators, including birds, crabs and starfish.

Limpet

You'll find these clamped to rocks when the tide is out. But when the tide is in, they crawl around, scraping algae off the rocks with their rough tongue.

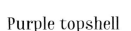

Purple topshell

This small sea snail has a pretty, striped shell. The colours fade as the snail gets older.

Molluscs

Orange-clubbed sea slug

You'll have to get down close to the water to spot this small sea slug. It grazes on the tiny creatures that live on seaweeds and rocks.

Blue-rayed limpet

These jewel-like limpets feed on seaweed found in rock pools that can only be reached when the tide is out. Remember to check tide times so you don't get caught by the incoming tide.

Spotted cowrie

A sea snail with three dark dots on its small, ridged shell. You're most likely to find it under stones.

Curled octopus

Look in large rock pools for this octopus. But even though it's quite big, you'll have to look carefully, because it changes colour to blend in with its surroundings.

Tentacles curl up when it's not moving

Common sea slug

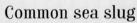

The size of a large carrot, these sea slugs slither across rock pools, looking for anemones to eat.

Little cuttlefish

A plump little cuttlefish with bulging eyes. Burrows into the sand at the bottom of rock pools, then changes colour to disguise itself.

13

Shellfish

Hermit crab

This crab finds empty shells to live in because it has a soft, fragile body. Whelk and cockle shells are popular, so they're a good place to start looking.

Right pincer larger than the left

Shore crab

A common crab with five little spikes on either side of its body. The shell is usually green but can sometimes be orange or red.

Females carry orange eggs on their belly

Brown shrimp

Most likely to be found on the sandy bottoms of rock pools. But you'll have to look carefully – their bodies are almost see-through.

Velvet swimming crab

This is a speedy crab with bright red eyes. Its body is covered in short hairs (but you'll get a nasty nip if you try to stroke it!)

Squat lobster

Look for them under stones and boulders. They have two long, brown claws with spikes along the inside.

Rock pool prawn

A large, see-through prawn with reddish-brown stripes. They're quick to dart for cover if you get too close.

Sea anemones and sea urchins

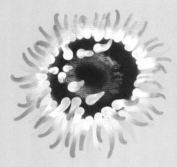

Dahlia anemone

This beautiful anemone uses its stinging tentacles to catch small fish and shellfish. Often reddish-brown, but can be anything from purple to yellow.

Edible sea urchin

Can be found in rock pools at very low tide. This large urchin grazes on seaweed and barnacles. Like other urchins, its spines drop off when it dies.

Its shell is called a test

Beadlet anemone

If you find this anemone above water, it looks just like a blob of red jelly. But when the tide comes in, the tentacles come out to catch small crabs and fish.

Elegant sea anemone

At low tide, the tentacles of this anemone hang limp like wet hair. Its colour varies from red, to pale grey-green.

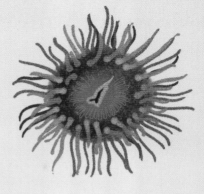

Often found on red algae

Purple sea urchin

Look closely for this large, deep-purple urchin that sits buried in the sand at the bottom of rock pools. Covered in pale spines.

Green sea urchin

This small urchin has strong, purple-tipped spines. You're most likely to spot it grazing on large seaweeds.

More rock pool life

Seashore springtail

Watch out for these tiny bugs creeping from crevices at low tide. They live in large groups, and swarm over rocks or float on water as they hunt for dead animals to eat.

Sea slater

Closely related to woodlice, these creatures emerge from under rocks late in the evening or at night to feed on seaweed.

Barnacle

Barnacles look like pale little bumps covering the rocks, but they're actually shellfish. When underwater, their 'legs' emerge to catch tiny scraps of food.

Tidepool copepod

These tiny creatures can be
seen in shallow rock pools
high up on the shore. Look
for orange specks darting
about in the water.

Green-leaf worm

Keep a lookout for this long,
emerald-green worm crawling
under rocks or around mussel
beds at low tide.

Oaten pipes hydroid

These bizarre, flower-like
creatures are found in
clusters. White tentacles
grow around their
mouths and catch
plankton (tiny sea
creatures) to eat.

19

Rock pool raiders

Ringed plover

This plump little bird hunts in shallow water. Watch it stand very still, then dart forward to nab an insect or small shellfish.

Oystercatcher

Listen for this wading bird's loud 'peep'-ing call. It prises open shellfish with its long, flat beak.

Herring gull

Look out for this large gull with a red spot on its beak. It visits rock pools to hunt for fish and shellfish, but might also try to pinch your lunch!

Ruddy turnstone

Found on rocky shores, this plucky bird flips over stones the size of its own body as it searches for food.

Summer colouring
(darker in winter)

Rock pipit

You'll see this bird on rocky coastlines, hopping and running from one stone to the next, hunting for insects and shellfish.

Otter

Wait until evening time for a chance to see this big, powerful hunter. As the sun sets, it scampers down to the shore to search for crabs and fish.

21

Spotting chart

Once you've spotted something from this book, find its sticker at the back and stick it on this chart in the space below its name.

Barnacle	Beadlet anemone	Bladder wrack	Blue-rayed limpet	Brown shrimp
Cockle	Common brittlestar	Common sea slug	Common starfish	Compass jellyfish
Coral weed	Corkwing wrasse	Curled octopus	Cushion star	Dahlia anemone
Dog whelk	Edible periwinkle	Edible sea urchin	Elegant sea anemone	Green-leaf worm
Green sea urchin	Gutweed	Hermit crab	Herring gull	Limpet

Little cuttlefish	Long-spined sea scorpion	Lumpfish	Mermaid's purse	Montagu's blenny
Moon jellyfish	Mussel	Oaten pipes hydroid	Orange-clubbed sea slug	Otter
Oystercatcher	Purple sea urchin	Purple topshell	Rainbow wrack	Ringed plover
Rock goby	Rock gunnel	Rock pipit	Rock pool prawn	Ruddy turnstone
Sea lettuce	Sea oak	Seashore springtail	Sea slater	Sea stickleback
Shanny	Shore clingfish	Shore crab	Shore rockling	Spiny starfish
Spotted cowrie	Squat lobster	Tidepool copepod	Velvet swimming crab	Worm pipefish

Index

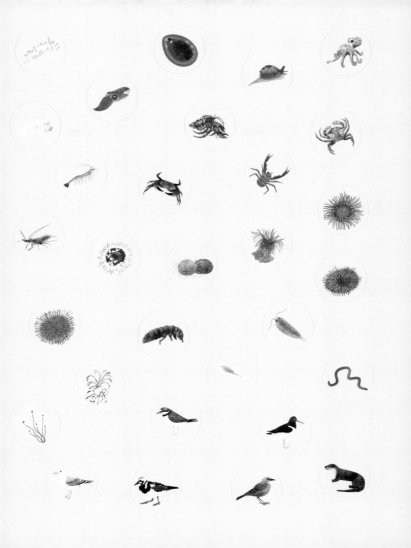